DINOSAURS
OF THE TRIASSIC ERA

JAN SOVAK

DOVER PUBLICATIONS
GARDEN CITY, NEW YORK

Note

The Triassic period, which began 248 million years ago, and ended 206 million years ago, fell directly after the largest extinction known! This was called the *Permian* extinction, in which about 95% of all the earth's species died out—and it was this extinction that made way for the first of the dinosaurs to appear! There were no dinosaurs at the very beginning of the Triassic period, but by the mid- to late Triassic they had begun to roam over the entire earth—and continued to do so for 160 million years. Triassic earth had a very hot and dry climate, with no ice at either the north or south poles. It was home to dinosaurs such as Blikanasaurus, Eoraptor, and Sellosaurus, along with the twenty-seven others found inside this coloring book. These dinosaurs, and others of the Triassic period were much smaller than the giants of the later periods. Most of them were carnivores, and bipedal—which means that they walked on two legs. No one knows exactly what noises these dinosaurs made, what color they were, how their skin felt, or how they behaved, but after studying the fossils of these impressive reptiles, scientists now understand more about their amazing prehistoric world. Just add color to Jan Sovak's beautiful illustrations, and read the fun dinosaur facts on each page to explore and experience for yourself the Triassic dinosaurs!

Copyright

Copyright © 2010 by Dover Publications
All rights reserved.

Bibliographical Note

Dinosaurs of the Triassic Era is a new work, first published by
Dover Publications in 2010.

International Standard Book Number

ISBN-13: 978-0-486-47265-2
ISBN-10: 0-486-47265-5

Manufactured in the United States of America
47265508   2022
www.doverpublications.com

The fossils of the *Agnosphitys* are some of the oldest ever found. Scientists are often in disagreement as to whether it is one of the very first dinosaurs, or a *dinosauromorph,* an ancient, reptilian-like creature that would have lived very close to the evolution of the dinosaurs.

Measuring about 25 feet in length, *Aliwalia* was the first of the larger-sized carnivorous dinosaurs. Because no other meat-eating dinosaur reached this size until millions of years later, it is considered the "grandfather" of the predatory giants. Its fossils were discovered in South Africa.

Although *Azendohsaurus* was considered a dinosaur for many years, it was recently determined to be an *archosauromorph*, an herbivorous reptile that bears many characteristics similar to the later herbivorous dinosaurs. It was named for the village of Azendoh, Morocco, which is located near a fossil deposit found in the Atlas Mountains.

The only *Blikanasaurus* fossils ever found were discovered in Cape Province, South Africa. Because only a single left limb was uncovered, very little information is known about this dinosaur. However, scientists estimate that it measured about ten feet in length, and had short, strong anklebones and large, forward pointing toes.

The fossils of a *Camposaurus* hind leg, and some cranial bones were discovered in Arizona. There is not much known about this dinosaur, but scientists estimate it to have been about 9 feet in length. Because its bones were hollow and very slim, it was probably a fast runner.

One of the first meat-eaters to live in North America, the incomplete fossilized *Caseosaurus* skeleton was uncovered in Texas. There is not much known about this dinosaur, but because many of the Triassic dinosaurs looked so similar to each other, it was probably small in size, with a long neck and a mouth full of sharp teeth. It was named for E. C. Case, a paleontologist.

Fossilized remains of *Chindesaurus*, whose name means "ghost-lizard," were found in Arizona, New Mexico, and Texas. It was about 6 feet long, and probably weighed around 70 pounds. It had a whip-like tail, long legs, and very sharp teeth.

The name *Coelophysis* means "hollow form," and refers to the hollow, thin bones that probably made this dinosaur a particularly fast runner. Discovered in the southwestern region of the United States, Coelophysis was the earliest dinosaur for which a complete fossilized skeleton has been found. It had very large eyes, and scientists believe it had good eyesight—useful when hunting the small lizard-like animals that were its prey.

Coloradisaurus lived in what is now the South American country of Argentina. It is known only from a fossilized skull, but scientists believe it to have been one of the few omnivorous dinosaurs of the Triassic. It had a small head and eyes, a short snout, and probably had a large body.

Considered the common ancestor of *all* dinosaurs, the name *Eoraptor* means "dawn-plunderer." It probably ate small, lizard-like animals, and used both its teeth and its claws to tear its prey. However, because it possessed both sharp and blunt teeth, there is a possibility that it was omnivorous. Several completed fossilized Eoraptor skeletons were found in Argentina, near the border of Chile.

Named after Gojira, the Japanese version of Godzilla, *Gojirasaurus* would have grown to be about 21 feet long and could have weighed up to 500 pounds. One of the larger Triassic dinosaurs, it got its name from a paleontologist who was a fan of the *Godzilla* movies! A fossilized tooth, four ribs, some vertebrae, and a few other bones were discovered in New Mexico.

Although a nearly complete fossilized *Herrerasaurus* skeleton was uncovered in Argentina in the late 1980s, the dinosaur was already known by fragmentary remains discovered some years earlier. It had a long tail, and a small head, and measured between 10 and 20 feet in length. It is interesting to note that Herrerasaurus had a special joint in its lower jaw that made its bite particularly powerful.

Isanosaurus was one of the very first herbivorous dinosaurs, as well as one of the first to walk with all four legs upon the ground. However, the claws on its front feet indicate that it was capable of standing on its back legs as well. Scientists believe that

Isanosaurus probably traveled in large herds in order to protect its young from predators, and it is the only dinosaur from the Triassic period whose fossils were discovered in Thailand.

Lagosuchus is best known for its tiny size, weighing no more than one pound. This *archosaur*—one of the early dinosaurs' closest relatives—had long,

slender legs and feet and was probably a very fast runner. Its fossilized remains were discovered in Argentina, and its name means "rabbit crocodile."

Measuring only 3 feet in length, *Lesothosaurus* was a small, bipedal dinosaur, as well as one of the few herbivores that lived during the Triassic period. It had a short, pointed snout that may have ended in a beak, as well as hind limbs that were much longer than its forelimbs. The remains of two fossilized Lesothosaurus' were found curled up together in South Africa, and scientists believe they may have been hibernating underground in order to escape the heat.

Lewisuchus was not a dinosaur, but a fast-moving, small reptile called a *thecodont*. Although a number of fossils were found in Argentina, it has been dis-covered that many of these actually belong to other animals, and so the exact size and appearance of Lewisuchus remains indefinite.

Liliensternus is identifiable by its five-fingered hands and narrow head. At 15 feet long, it was one of the larger predators of its time, and might have preyed on smaller dinosaurs as well as lizard-like animals. Its fossilized remains were discovered in Germany, and it takes its name from a German scientist.

Although very dinosaur-like in appearance, *Marasuchus* was actually a *dinosauromorph*—a direct ancestor of the dinosaurs. Its fossils were found in South America, and there is evidence that it lived in Europe as well. It was lightweight, with long hind legs and a long tail.

One of the largest dinosaurs of the Triassic period, the herbivorous *Melanosaurus* grew to be about 40 feet long. It walked on all four legs, and resembled a somewhat smaller version of the herbivorous giants of the later periods.

Mussaurus, whose name means "mouse-lizard" is known only from fossilized remains of the eggs and infants of its species. Because of this, it is impossible to determine the exact size it would have been as an adult, but scientists estimate that Mussaurus could have grown to be about 10 feet long. The infant skeletons found were only about 6 inches in length.

Pisanosaurus was a Triassic herbivore, whose appearance can be estimated based on a partial skeleton found in Argentina. It was a small dinosaur, measuring only about 3 feet long and 1 foot high. Fossilized tailbones were not recovered, but scientists believe its tail was about the same length as its body.

Plateosaurus was one of the most common and widespread Triassic dinosaurs, with its fossilized remains being found in over 50 different locations. It had a long tail, measuring about half its body length, and a claw on its thumb that may have allowed it a firm hold on trees while feeding. It could have also been used for defense against predators.

Considered the ancestor to the well-known Jurrassic dinosaur, *Comsognathus*, *Procompsognathus*, was identified by fossilized remains found in Germany. Although the remains were badly damaged, scientists believe this dinosaur was about 4 feet long with small, sharp teeth, and probably ate insects and lizards.

Protoavis, whose name means "first-bird," was an *archosaur* that had features resembling a bird's. Scientists are unsure if it could fly, and do not classify it as a bird. Many Protoavis fossils have been found, including a complete skeleton in Texas. It had small teeth on the tip of its jaw, and because its eyes were located at the front of its skull, it probably led a nocturnal lifestyle.

24

The herbivore *Riojasaurus* was named after the La Rioja province in Argentina, where its fossils were discovered. It had a long neck, a heavy, rounded body, and a thick tail and legs. It probably walked on all fours, but would have been capable of standing on its hind legs for short periods of time.

Saturnalia is the oldest-known true dinosaur to have walked the earth, existing about 227 million years ago. It would have been about the size of small deer, and probably ate plants. Saturnalia is named after a Roman festival, and is considered a primitive ancestor to the giant herbivores of the Jurrasic period.

Unlike most Triassic dinosaurs, an abundance of *Sellosaurus* fossils have been found—including 20 completed or nearly completed skeletons in Germany. It had strong legs, and claws on its thumbs that would have been useful either for self-defense or for obtaining food.

Discovered in Brazil, the only remains of *Staurikosaurus* found were the fossilized lower-jaw, spine, legs, and some teeth. The exact size and shape of this dinosaur's body can only be estimated, but it is believed to have been small in size, and a carnivore. The Staurikosaurus had a special hinge on its jaw that allowed it to move both up and down, as well as backwards and forwards.

Syntarsus was a lightly built, fast-moving dinosaur. It had hollow bones and a crest on its head. It lived in what is now Zimbabwe, Africa. Syntarsus ate fish and lizard-like animals, and probably lived in herds. Because of the proportion of its back legs to its front legs, it may have moved by hopping, rather than running, and some scientists believe that its body was covered in feathers.

Fossils of the *Thecodontosaurus* were found in England and Wales. It had a large head, short neck, large eyes, and blunt teeth. It had narrow hands with extended claws on each of its five-fingers useful for obtaining food. Thecodontosaurus was an herbivore, and had a tail that was much larger than its body.